Marine Monsters

Sticker Activity Fun

Written by **Gordon Volke**

TOP THAT! Kids™

Copyright © 2005 Top That! Publishing plc
25031 W. Avenue Stanford, Suite #60, Valencia, CA 91355
Top That! Kids is a trademark of
Top That! Publishing plc
All rights reserved

Count the Sea Creatures

Here are the names and pictures of some well-known underwater creatures. Can you...

Say each name?
Say how many you can see of each one?
Write the number in words by tracing over the dotted outline?

1 one
Blue Whale

2 two
Killer Whales

3 three
Manta Rays

4 four
Swordfish

5 five
Hammerhead Sharks

6 six
Squid

7 seven
Barracuda

8 eight
Scorpion Fish

9 nine
Horseshoe Crabs

10 ten
Box Jellyfish

An Amazing Escape!

An Underwater Maze

Once you have placed the stickers on the maze, see if you can safely guide the tuna to safety. The mako shark is hungry and has spotted a tasty-looking tuna. There is only one escape route for the tuna to reach the rocky cave in which to hide.

Put a sticker here

When you have finished going around the maze, record the route the tuna has taken.

Going through the underwater maze, the tuna followed these directions:
It turned left .... times.
It turned right .... times.
It went straight ahead ...... times.

Go Straight
Turn Left
Turn Right

Did You Know That?
Some species of shark can smell just one drop of blood in one million drops of sea water.

Put a sticker here

Put a sticker here

HOME

Who is Heavy?

By completing this puzzle you will learn about weighing things.

If you weigh something small and light, you measure that weight in ounces. This is written oz for short.

If you weigh something big and heavy, you measure it in pounds (which is equal to 16 ounces). Pounds are written lbs for short.

Now look at this picture. Three of the named things in it are small and light; the other three are big and heavy. Decide which is which. Then put the stickers marked oz beside the small, light ones, and the lbs stickers beside the big, heavy ones.

Remember
Use oz (ounces) for small, light things, and lbs (pounds) for big, heavy things.

Tuna
I am one of the largest and fastest marine fish, and can swim up to 90 mph

Put a sticker here

Seahorse
I am a small creature with a horse-shaped head.

Put a sticker here

Who is Light?

Whale Shark
I am the largest fish in the world and can grow up to 50 ft long.

Put a sticker here

Great White Shark
I have about 3,000 teeth and can grow up to 23 ft long.

Put a sticker here

Hermit Crab
I am a small crustacean with no backbone. I eat worms and plankton.

Put a sticker here

Shrimp
I am a tiny crustacean with a long tail and a pair of pincers.

Put a sticker here

7

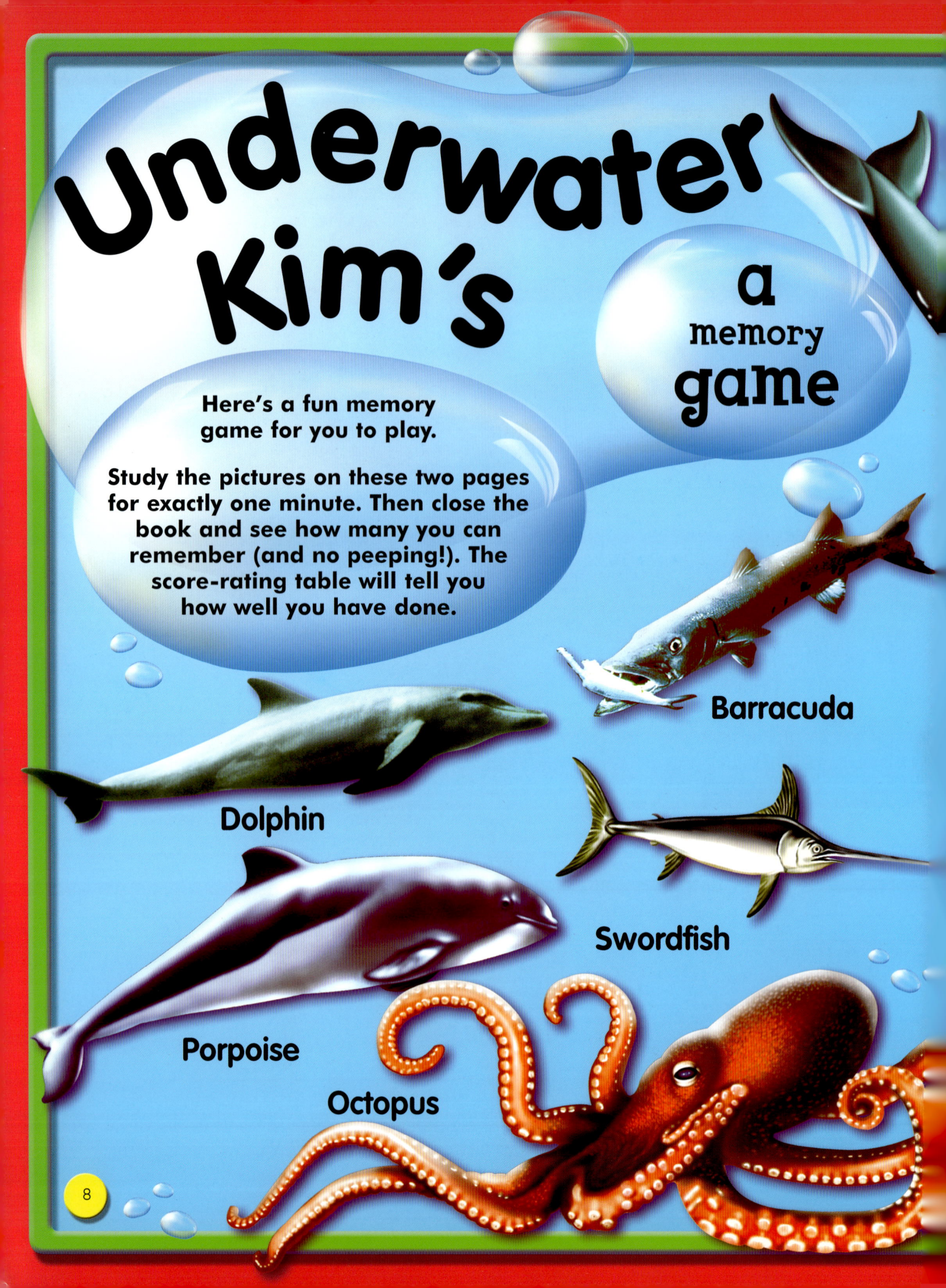

Underwater Kim's a memory game

Here's a fun memory game for you to play.

Study the pictures on these two pages for exactly one minute. Then close the book and see how many you can remember (and no peeping!). The score-rating table will tell you how well you have done.

Barracuda

Dolphin

Swordfish

Porpoise

Octopus

Tuna

Flying Fish

Blue Whale

Killer Whale

Great White Shark

Hammerhead Shark

Manta Ray

Score Ratings

0-3   remembered. Try again!

4-6   remembered. That's pretty good!

7-9   remembered. Excellent!

9-12 remembered. Fantastic! Amazing! (Sure you didn't peep?)

9

A Whale's Tale

Read this story on your own or with the help of an adult. Write the missing words in the spaces, copying the correct spellings. Then talk about the questions at the end.

Hello! My name's Barnacle, but you can call me Barney. My little sister does. She's called Marina.

I'm a humpback whale. Why don't you come to visit me in my underwater world? It's very calm and peaceful... most of the time!

I'm swimming along the coast at the moment. I have to be careful not to go too near the beaches, or I can get _____. Marina did once, but she was lucky.
She was carried back out to sea by the _____.

Watch this. I'm going to dive down to deep water now.
See how my _____ sticks right up into the air.
People like to see that.
They take photos of me with their _____.

goodbye   tail   stuck   cameras   tide   two

UH-OH! I hear a big boat coming. I hope the people on it aren't going to chase me and shoot at me with a big spear. My brother Rorke was caught like that. I never saw him again. No, it's okay. It's a passenger boat and the people are friendly.

Shall we make a big splash? I love doing this. Ready? One, _____, three - JUMP! We're leaping right out of the water, like dolphins do. They don't make a splash half as big as mine!

What's that? You have to go now? Oh, okay. I've enjoyed sharing the sea with you today. Mind how you go. _____!

1 Would you like to be a whale? Say why... or why not.

2 Do you think whales should be hunted by people? Say what you think.

3 Find out more about humpback whales for yourself.

How Very Odd!

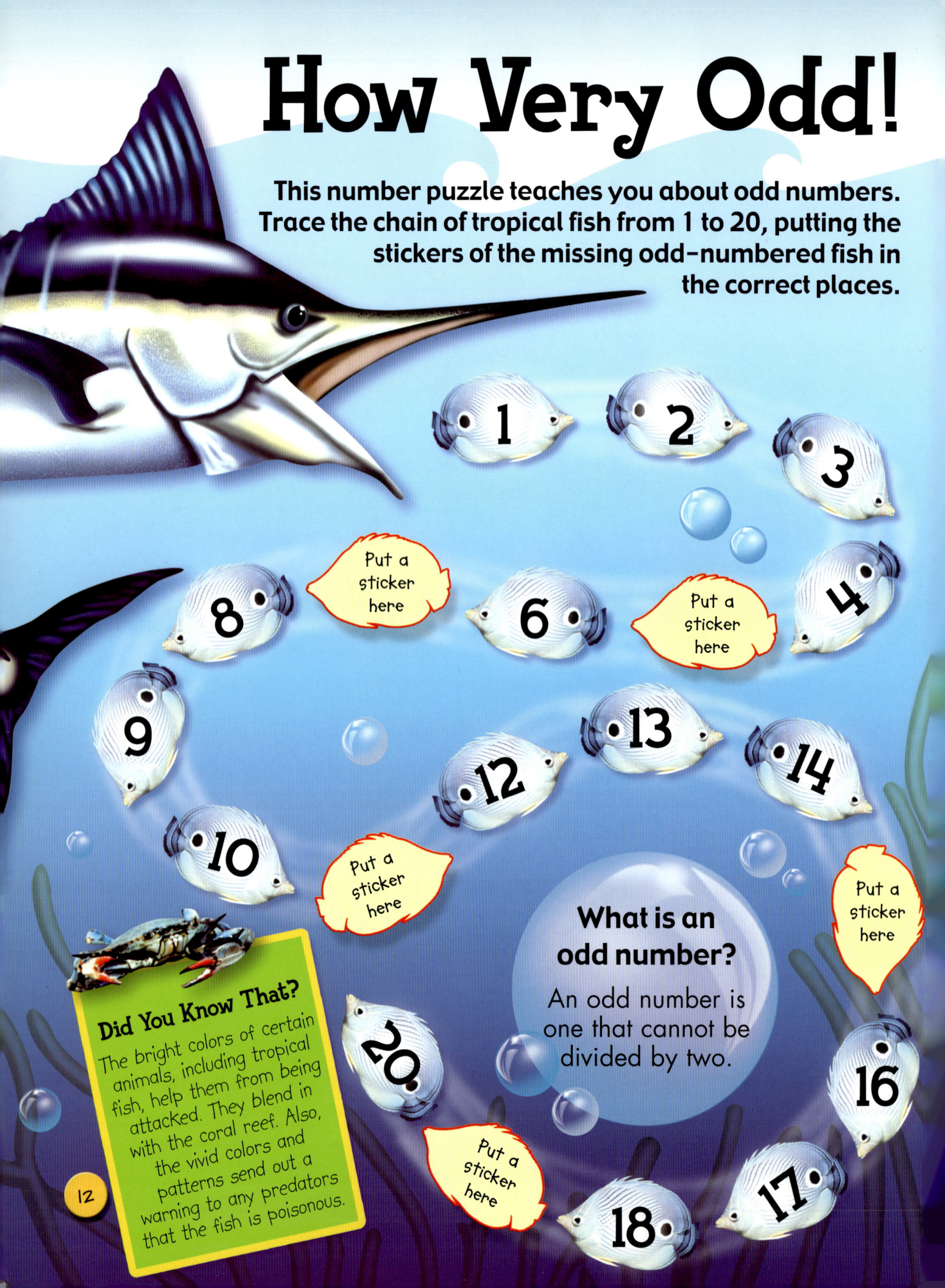

This number puzzle teaches you about odd numbers. Trace the chain of tropical fish from 1 to 20, putting the stickers of the missing odd-numbered fish in the correct places.

What is an odd number?

An odd number is one that cannot be divided by two.

Did You Know That?

The bright colors of certain animals, including tropical fish, help them from being attacked. They blend in with the coral reef. Also, the vivid colors and patterns send out a warning to any predators that the fish is poisonous.

Stickers for page 13

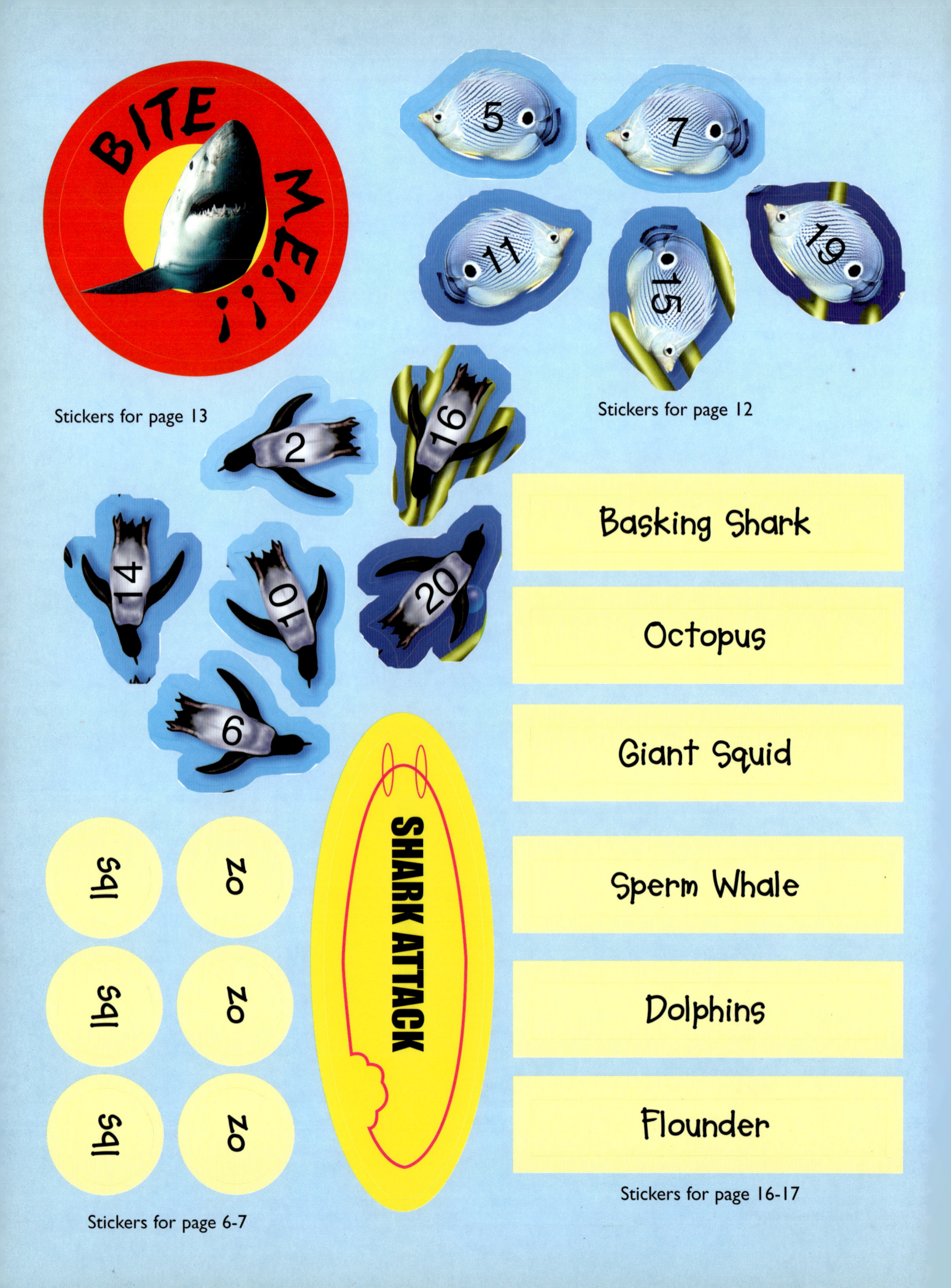

Stickers for page 12

Basking Shark

Octopus

Giant Squid

Sperm Whale

Dolphins

Flounder

SHARK ATTACK

Stickers for page 16-17

Stickers for page 6-7

Stickers for page 5

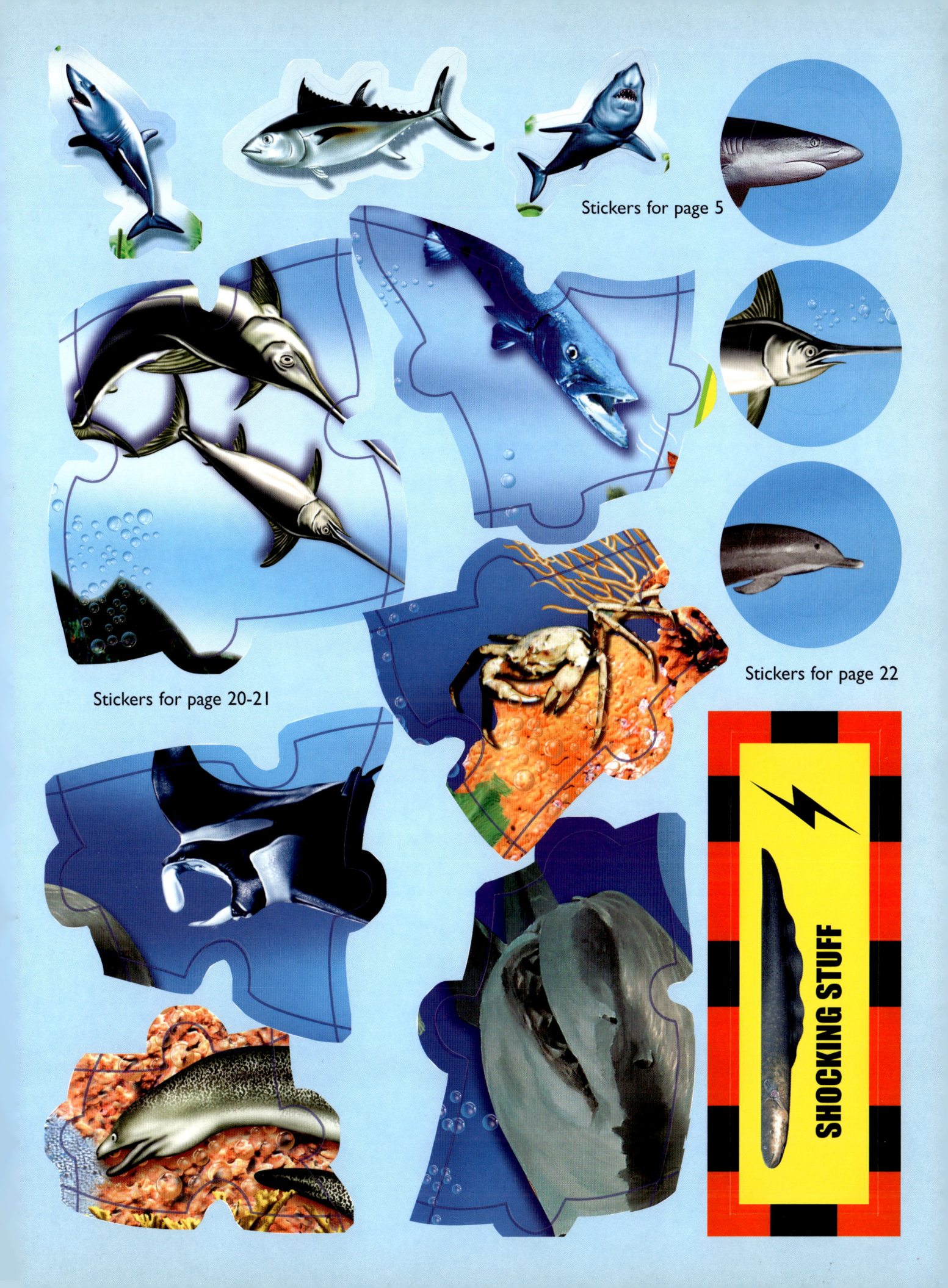

Stickers for page 20-21

Stickers for page 22

SHOCKING STUFF

Even it Out

The puzzle on this page teaches you about even numbers. Look at the seal trying to catch some of the penguins. Four of them with even numbers on their backs are missing. Can you put the matching penguin stickers in the correct places?

What is an even number?

An even number is one that can be divided by two.

Did You Know That?

Seagulls are greedy birds. They will eat almost anything. As well as fish from the sea, they feed on shellfish and the eggs of other birds. They pick up waste thrown from ships, and scavenge on rubbish tips inland. They also follow tractors, eating the worms and grubs turned up in the ploughed soil.

13

Me and My Shadow

Using a pencil, draw lines to join these six sea creatures with their matching outlines. Then ask an adult to read you the fascinating facts about each one. To get you started, we've drawn in the first one for you!

Manta Ray
Like whales and basking sharks, these gentle giants feed on tiny sea creatures called plankton. They glide through the water, flapping their fins like huge underwater birds.

Dolphin
Baby dolphins are born underwater. Their mothers have to carry them to the surface to help them take their first breath of air.

Shark
Sharks may be very scary, but they do a good job. They help to clean up the sea by eating up all the dead and dying underwater animals.

Crab
Crabs have hard, horny shells to protect them from attack. They feed and defend themselves with their pincers, which give a very powerful nip.

Moray Eel
There are about 100 species of moray eels living in the coral reefs or rocky areas of shallow tropical seas. They have long, muscular, snake-like bodies. Camouflaged moray eels hide among their surroundings waiting for their prey, which they find by using their keen sense of smell.

Octopus
These animals are very clever. Scientists have proved this by teaching captured octopuses to recognize colors and choose different things.

15

Where do I Live?

Here are six sea creatures and some facts about where they live in the sea. You have to study these facts and then decide which animal is which. Place the name stickers in the place shown beside each one when you know.

Put a sticker here

I swim near the surface of the sea so I can feed on the plankton living there.

Put a sticker here

I am a flat fish that burrows in the sand at the bottom of the sea. The markings on my back make it really hard to see me.

Put a sticker here

I am a gentle, shy creature with eight legs who likes to hide in rocks and caves, out of everyone's way.

16

Put a sticker here

We are happy, clever sea creatures who like to leap out of the water into the sunshine. It is called breaching.

Put a sticker here

I am a big whale that can dive down into deep water to catch giant squid. They are my favorite meal.

Put a sticker here

I am a strange creature with ten legs that nobody knows much about. I live in some of the deepest parts of the ocean.

17

Marine Monsters

The puzzle on this page is quite easy. The one on the opposite page is a bit more difficult.

Using a pencil, join the dots in both pictures, starting at number 1 and going on upward until you reach the last number. Then color your completed picture with crayons, marker pens or gel-pens, using the photograph to guide you.

Can you read the names of these two marine monsters? How much more can you find out about them?

Dot to Dot

Sea Lion
Male sea lions have between 3 and 20 mates. Baby sea lions, called pups, are born amidst huge crowds of other sea lions, all sharing the same rocks. These massive groups are called colonies.

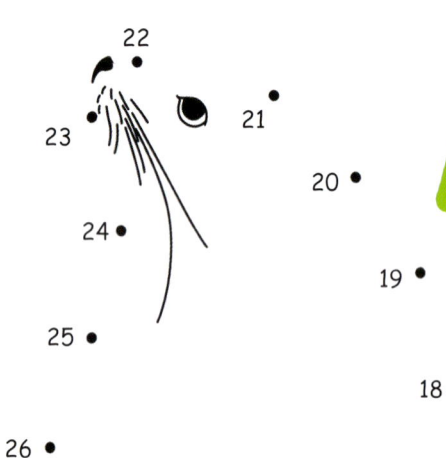

Killer Whale

These huge black-and-white creatures known as orcas are not really whales at all. They are dolphins—the largest member of the dolphin family. They live in groups that vary in size from only a few to as many as 50.

19

A Sticker Jigsaw

These two pages are lots of fun! Use the jigsaw-shaped stickers to complete this colorful underwater scene of a beautiful coral reef.

Put a sticker here

Put a sticker here

Put a sticker here

20

Put a sticker here

Put a sticker here

Put a sticker here

Did You Know That?

Coral reefs look as if they are made of rocks, but in fact the "stones" that you see are millions of different animals with stone-like skins—all living together in one place. In other words, a coral reef is alive!

21

Long-distance Race

The dolphin, the great white shark and the swordfish are having a race. They want to know who can cross the ocean first by traveling the shortest distance. You can see the route that each one chose to take. Now you have to measure them!

Ask an adult to cut you a length of wool or string. Then place the thread along each line, going round any curves, until you reach the end of the line. Pinching the string where the line ends, take the string off and measure it against the side of the ruler below.

How far did the dolphin travel?
How far did the great white shark travel?
How far did the swordfish travel?

Which animal used the shortest distance and won the race?

Dolphin

Great White Shark

Swordfish

Put a sticker here

Put a sticker here

Put a sticker here

1ST
2ND
3RD

☐ in.

☐ in.

☐ in.

QUIZ TIME

How much can you remember about Marine Monsters? Find out by tackling this quick-fire quiz.

1. In how much sea water can some sharks detect one drop of blood?
   a) one thousand drops   b) one hundred drops   c) one million drops

2. Which one of these is the odd-one-out and why?
   a) Great White   b) Basking   c) Humpback
   d) Hammerhead   e) Tiger

3. Sperm whales dive into very deep water to hunt their favorite food, giant squid.
   a) Correct?   b) Wrong?

4. Divide these numbers into two groups, one odd and one even—2 3 4 5 6 7 8 9

5. What is the other name for a killer whale?
   a) Orca   b) Porpoise   c) Fred

6. Whales, basking sharks, and manta rays feed on millions of tiny animals that float in the sea. What are these little animals called?
   a) Fish   b) Plankton   c) Planks

7. An octopus gets its name because it looks like a cat.
   a) Correct?   b) Wrong?

8. Can you complete this sentence?
   "Baby dolphins are born - - - - - - - - - -".

9. What is a barracuda?
   a) An ice-cream   b) A type of boat
   c) A long, thin fish with lots of sharp teeth

10. What is the first thing that a mother dolphin has to do when a baby dolphin is born?

Answers

1. b) One million
2. c) Humpback (This is a whale. The others are types of sharks).
3. a) Correct
4. Odd—3, 5, 7 and 9. Even—2, 4, 6 and 8.
5. a) Orca
6. b) Plankton
7. b) Wrong (Octopus means "with eight legs").
8. Underwater
9. c) A long, thin fish with lots of sharp teeth.
10. Take the baby to the surface for its first breath of air.

24